RESTLESS

REALM

It's not just the spirits that are uneasy

By

Barry R. Frankish

With over twenty-five years experience in the paranormal field, Barry R Frankish is also a co-host on *The Pure Paranormal Radio Show*, an award winning online radio show hosted by his good friend Tom Warrington. In his first book, the Doncaster-based paranormal researcher swaps microphone for pen and paper to share not just his thoughts towards the paranormal and those who work under its umbrella term, but to also give a little insight for those new to the field into what awaits those curious enough to enter.

Not forgetting a few true stories along the way, local to his hometown.

The paranormal realm
More questions than answers

Do we truly know what we are talking about?

GHOST

Noun: an apparition of a dead person which is believed to appear in visual form to the living, typically as a nebulous image.

The above are the definitions of a ghost, as explained by name of dictionary, but what is the reality what a ghost really is? Some perceive a ghost is a conscious entity come back from the dead for reasons we have yet to fathom; others believe they are nothing more than nonconscious replays caught up in a never-ending loop caused by some traumatic event. Whatever they are, we are still no closer to understanding why many people from all over the world and from all backgrounds still to this day claim to come into contact with these otherworldly entities. So will we ever truly come to understand what a ghost is and why so many people at some point in their lives come into contact with them? Probably not in our lifetime.

Looking for and finding evidence are two different things and in this day and age it is becoming more and more difficult especially as we have at our disposal the technology to alter and manipulate photos almost instantly making the confirmation of any submitted evidence difficult to authenticate and as we all know taking someone's testimonial without the support of physical proof will always be taken at the discretion of those it is aimed towards and seeing as technology is progressing faster than our ability to understand its original purpose we are going to find extremely difficult to get anything submitted seriously enough to warrant serious investigation.

GHOST

I wander around from place to place
With an haunted look upon my face
Everything around has changed so much
I reach out for you, it's just an icy touch
I look in on you once in a while
Remembering a long forgotten memory, to make you smile
My body may be gone, and my spirit free
To hold you once more, my only plea
Lurking in the shadows, staying out of the way
The angels come take me, is what I pray
Until that time, when God decides
A ghost I remain in the darkness, hides.

Barry R Frankish

A little about the author

To be honest there's not much to tell. I was born in Hemsworth West Yorkshire, UK England in January 1971.

Brought up and schooled in the mining town of Featherstone, West Yorkshire, my childhood was primarily what you'd expect of living in a mining environment, in the sense of kids would normally make up their own entertainment by playing street football, rugby or just staying out all day doing whatever until we were called in by our parents. My father worked for British Rail manning the local signal box, which at the time was deemed very modern, using an electronic and push buttons instead of the traditional lever operated system. Sometimes I was able to accompany him to work. My mother was an housewife basically looking after me and my two brothers and looking after the home.

My grandparents lived in a small village close to the city of York, which is deemed as one of the most haunted cities in the UK, if not *the* most haunted city. This meant that I was lucky enough to spend a lot of my childhood visiting the city, getting to know it both in a geographical sense and the reputation of its history and stories of times past. One example of these that captured my imagination is of a small terrier breed of dog that was bricked up somewhere in the Minster by a jealous work colleague of the animal's owner. So distraught was the dog's owner he offered a whole years wages for the safe return of his faithful friend, but they were sadly never reunited. It is said that the dog can still be heard whimpering within the Minster to this day.

Growing up in the 1970s as far as I can remember my family never had any paranormal incidents, if they did I never got any knowledge of them. My father in one way gave me the ability to see reason and the seriousness behind a situation and my mother gave me empathy, a sense of humour and artistic attributes as well as an interest in that was is different or somewhat unusual because in my opinion my mother possesses a far more open mind than my father ever did which in my opinion is a necessity within paranormal circles.

I became interested in the paranormal I dare say from an early age what with watching films such as the Hammer House of Horrors series as well as Tales of the Unexplained and even though they were not directly paranormal they added fuel to my fire.

My interest then stemmed to books with the works of Arthur C Clarke and his World of Strange Powers which for me these books were perfect because such publications had everything under one roof so to say because they didn't just cover one subject but multiple and from all over the world from all eras. I cannot lie because as far as I am aware I have never seen a full blown apparition even though I have experienced some odd unexplainable things, one being on a school residential trip which I go into a little later on. In all honesty even though I have a vast interest in all that is paranormal my experiences have been limited and I am not the kind to exaggerate to get people to show interest in myself or my work.

The only qualifications I hold are those I've achieved through schooling, higher education and employment-based learning. I do not hold anything that qualifies me as an professional or expert within the paranormal field. I believe that any structured qualification in a field that is based on theory, speculation and unquantifiable accounts is difficult, if not impossible. Don't get me wrong, there are experts and professionals in areas such as photography, sound and lighting that can assist you in your search for paranormal evidence, but when it comes to the paranormal itself, there are no experts – only people with more experience of researching and directly searching for the unknown. There are no governing bodies to hand out certificates stating that you are a professional paranormal investigator when you reach a requirement of hours for research. Take driving as an example: driving for ten years doesn't make you a better driver than someone who has just passed their test. In fact, it can lead to picking up bad habits and becoming complacent in their actions.

It is my belief that the real qualifications within the paranormal realm are gained from learning from other researchers, listening to their advice and guidance, analysing the findings of others and offering constructive criticism when things seem less than concrete. And sometimes it also means denouncing another's work if their findings are proven to be untrue.

Even with the society of today being a lot more diverse in beliefs and unbiased than it was, say, one hundred years ago, people are still wary when coming forward with reports and accounts of the unknown or unusual. This is mostly due to the ridicule that could follow, the desire not to want to be labelled as "weird", as incapable of being able to process situations logically or, worse, mentally unbalanced – especially since once you are handed a label or reputation, it is very difficult to shake off.

Many people these days do consider themselves to be open minded, but how open minded are they really, especially in front of family, friends and work colleagues? Ask someone if they believe in ghosts, and a large percentage will say no; not because they truly believe their answer, but out of fear of what others may think. It is sometimes easier to hide their beliefs than risk ridicule from those they like and respect. On the other hand, ask an audience if they believe in God, or gods and goddesses, and many will answer yes without hesitation. So why should this be any different? Perhaps, the only difference is what society deems acceptable.

I don't mean any disrespect in this. Although I don't have any strong religious beliefs myself, I understand those who find comfort in the form of a higher entity, and I have a huge amount of respect for other's beliefs and opinions, especially on the subject of religion. Millions of people, worldwide, believe in entities that they have never seen and are quite willing to build churches and temples to worship, and even fight in their names, and hardly anyone questions their motives or sanity. But, once again, asked if they believe in ghosts and you will still get a mixed reaction. Surely one should complement the other. For example, the Bible teaches of the holy ghost and spiritual visitations.

Why do people see what they believe to be ghosts and what sort of people see them? It seems anyone can see a ghost and many who do see them either don't know they've seen a ghost or are so closed to the idea they choose not to acknowledge what they have experienced, denying it. Living in today's busy world is very easy to do due to the fact our lives constantly see us running around chasing our own proverbial tails, what with work pressures, the cost of living, sees our minds constantly in stress mode and many of us find it hard to switch off and relax so is it any wonder our spiritual side plays second fiddle to our everyday lives?

"Seek and ye shall find", the passage from the Bible, Matthew 7:7, means your 'efforts will be rewarded' and in many cases hard work and effort does pay off, but that is not always the case. This is more so within the paranormal, because to date no one has yet come forward with any sort of credible conclusive evidence to prove the existence of an afterlife, even though many have tried to claim that title.

Paranormal research isn't like any other hobby or interest because there is no end product to show for your efforts; it's all speculation and theory, whereas with other interests there may be physical rewards such as finds as in archaeology, or items to store such as keepsakes. The paranormal does not offer such mementos: in fact if anything you'll probably find yourself a little light in the wallet or purse purchasing items you think you might need but won't end up using, or regret buying. Despite the many items that are currently on the market claiming otherwise, there is no product that is designed to detect or capture images of ghosts. How can any item claim that, when it is impossible to prove their existence?

Everyone alive today possesses the ability to see a ghost, though as mentioned previously many choose to ignore their senses and only choose to accept what is physically there. The choice to deny this could stem from anything from childhood trauma to how their religious teachings have integrated themselves into their lives, or they simply don't believe -whatever the reason it's not for us to judge, but we all possess the ability to connect with the spirit world in one way or the other.

We've all at some point found something when we weren't looking for it - be it a ten pound note in the pocket of a pair of jeans or something we misplaced at some point in our lives only for it to turn up out of the blue. That's how the paranormal works, it doesn't stick to the conventional, it's totally the opposite: in this case it's "seek and ye won't find" and more "Boo, here I am" Programmes such as the ghost hunting shows you see on TV or online, none of them have captured anything that could be considered groundbreaking in regards to credible evidence, and the majority of the locations used will bear no fruit. This is because these programmes are for entertainment, and full investigations are more than sixty minutes worth of looking around. Full investigations are based on weeks, months and sometimes years of being present in a single location, with a lot of effort made from a full team of investigators, with none of the considerations being ratings and entertainment value. A lot of programmes are there for the novelty of showing a new locations, which they can tick off of their to-do lists, and straight onto the next. What I'm getting at here, is that it's not us who find them, but them who find us.

Does a person need to believe in ghosts to experience one?....Quick answer 'no'

Over the years the most credible experiences have been witnessed by individuals who have held no interest whatsoever in the paranormal, which to me gives a lot more credibility to an account due to the lack of attentiveness towards the field.

Take this account for example: The Treasurer's House York, England 1953. Apprentice-plumber, Harry Martindale, who was 18 at the time, was tasked with fitting new pipes in the cellar of this building. Having set himself up a working platform, he promptly set to work. Perched on his ladder, he began to hear some peculiar sounds which he attributed to the workers upstairs; but as it got louder he began having doubts, and soon came to the realisation this was not music he was hearing, but in fact the blasts of a trumpet. This sound soon became deafening and as Harry looked down he witnessed what could only be described as a plumed helmet come into view. He then watched an entire legion of Roman soldier, complete with horses and weaponry, march within feet of his position. What gave this story even more credibility was of all the soldiers and horses witnessed that day, not one could be seen below the knee – and it was later discovered that the original ground level was feet below the floor that he could see and was working on. Also, what he described was not your stereotypical or well-documented Roman soldiers with metal armour, but when it was looked into, his description accurately fitted documented description of the soldiers of that time, even down to the swords they carried.

Harry wasn't the sort of person to go to the papers; quite the opposite, as he didn't mention this to anyone at first in case of ridicule. When he did go public, Harry was accused of making up the whole story, but he stuck to his guns and in the 1990's, during further works, the remains of the original Roman road were discovered, right where Harry had stated it was. Archaeological findings also confirmed that the uniforms Harry described were also accurate, as those that used that particular road were soldiers conscripted from local tribes and integrated into the legion, often with their own weapons and uniforms. After this came to light, Harry was seen in a new light as people started to believe his experience was genuine. Even after all of this, Harry still had no interest in the paranormal, and just wanted others to know of what he had experienced.

In my opinion, it is an experience that is worth looking into if you have an interest in the paranormal field.

As previously mentioned many of those who have paranormal experiences do so out of the blue and are totally unexpected, whereas those who purposely look for activity very rarely find what they are seeking and in many instances unintentionally attribute natural phenomena such as noises and smells even shadows as paranormal when realistically they are not and can be quite easily dismissed; but because of the mindset and, sometimes, a desperateness for results the very things we know to be normal becomes in some people's minds quite the opposite. You get many types of people from all walks of life, some of which are more susceptible towards the spirit world whereas others are not, but why do some experience such interactions and others don't? Could it be down to a certain mindset making the recipient more open to suggestion? I mean, we all know people who are a little easier to persuade or maybe it's chemical imbalances within the brain causing some kind of illusionary vision and because the brain cannot rationalise the message it has received from the eyes it puts it in to a category we can understand, resulting in what we would consider to be the image of a ghost. At some point we have all heard someone call out our name and in most cases it is because another individual requests our attention but hearing what we consider is someone calling our name is also another form of tinnitus which is more common than people realise that can contribute to what I consider audio pareidolia due to imbalances within in the ear canal or drum causing random sounds to be recognised as a familiar voice or sound.

These are just a couple of possible explanations into how we could misinterpret information; there are others too to consider, but I'm the last person to tell you how someone's brain works, especially since I can't understand how my own little piece of grey matter works.

There are also other factors to consider too, such as an individual's mental state, which must also be considered: for example, are there signs of stress which too can contribute to brain chemistry imbalances? Even stress and fatigue must be taken in to consideration when it comes to investigating reporters of ghost sightings, more so when interviewing witnesses.

This doesn't mean that experiences are not real just because someone is stressed or tired, but it needs to be taken into account when conducting an investigation.

One subject I would like to touch upon is that of suggestive hauntings. What I mean by that is, for example, if I told enough people that a particular area or building was haunted, even if no paranormal occurrences had ever been reported at that location, would it encourage activity to manifest itself through suggestion alone?

It may sound strange, but it is one of the questions that needs to be considered during paranormal research. In the way that fear and panic can spread amongst a populous, moving from person to person, it can work the same way with hauntings. Suggestion can be a very powerful tool, one that can be helpful (for example, being more aware of possible signs of danger), but it can also distort the perception of experiences. Mentioning that a certain sound has been heard, for example, footsteps, would make another person more likely to assume that distant sounds could possibly be footsteps as well; or saying that you had seen a dark figure, could lead someone to believe that a flickering shadow was the same dark figure. On some paranormal shows, for instance, the main character panics and screams, which causes the rest of the crew to respond by dropping everything and running in all directions, without even knowing why they are running.

IT'S NOTHING LIKE THE TV SHOWS

Anyone with an interest in the paranormal will at some point sat down and watched a typical generic ghost hunting TV show. You probably know the type: the main host or hosts, followed around in the dark by a camera crew calling out "is there anyone there? Knock once for yes, knock twice for no". Don't get me wrong, there's nothing wrong with actually watching these types of programmes for a little light entertainment. But it's important to remember that is all they are "entertainment", something to pass away half an hour or so, and not necessarily to be taken seriously. A ghost hunt and an investigation are two totally different concepts. Take ghost hunting for a start: a dozen or so people, sometimes not known to each other, turn up at a location armed with a torch, and maybe a few other little bits of paraphernalia they've seen used on TV shows. They are then broken up into small teams and sent to different areas within that location to do exactly what they've seen on TV, and a few hours later and after a few snacks and some reminiscing about the areas they have covered, they say their goodbyes and go home. That's a ghost hunt.

An investigation on the other hand is a totally different kettle of fish and is aimed at the more serious investigator or researcher: this is where time and patience is required, as well as an eye for detail and inaccuracies. Firstly, the investigator or researcher is normally contacted by the owner or resident of the property, after experiencing inexplicable occurrences, and, for whatever reason, they are looking for answers as to why these events are happening. They will contact researchers that they have, perhaps, been recommended to and believe are experienced enough to possibly give them the answers they need. Working with those with good reputations in the field lowers the risk of finding those whose motives aren't precisely genuine.

Once contact has been established and if both parties agree and once ground rules have been set in place with regards to movement also equipment used and duration of any experiments that are felt necessary the investigation can be put into motion. This is the beginning of the differences from a ghost hunt, as questions must be asked. Interviewing witnesses allows you to get a thorough assessment of what has been experienced, including dates and times, and also helps ascertain their state of mind and general mental wellbeing, as well as any hidden motives. Doing a thorough walk around the building or buildings in daylight can help you visualise easier the events that have taken place. Walking around the external of the buildings allows you to gain information on any possible natural external interference that could cause unusual phenomenon. Bearing in mind the location of structures, for example, rural or urban, allows you to take into account any animals in the area or the amount of traffic on roads that could have some bearing on the investigation. Even structures such as electricity pylons and water pipes have been known to interfere with findings, especially if you are the type of person who feels better using technology to aid you in your quest such as temperature loggers that register the ambient temperature and not surface temperature which is unintentionally misunderstood as room temperature. Also notice the little things, too, such as temperature fluctuations and draughts, and possible physical reasons for these. And not forgetting the age-old haunted house favourite, the creaky floorboards - it may sound like a cliché, but they do exist, as do unbalanced doors which unexpectedly open on their own at two in the morning, not because a ghost or spirit is opening them but because of internal temperature changes within the property causes items such as wooden doors and window frames to expand and contract, giving the impression that something or someone is interfering with them.

Taking the information you have accumulated, and with full permission, go deeper find out as much as you possibly can regarding the property, especially information about previous residents or workforce. I'd recommend that you make use of your local library, especially their archive departments to identify what was there on that land before. It is always best to look for the normal before you search for the paranormal: once you've established that natural and human factors are irrelevant to the experiences that have been reported to you, start looking at the history of the haunting and sightings. It may be that there has been significant activity at certain times of the year – these are known as anniversary ghosts, where entities seem to appear at times such as Christmas, birthdays, and even anniversaries, hence the terminology. It is also useful to look at occurrences such as deaths at the property. Many unusual experiences are connected to sudden deaths, especially if an individual met an untimely demise such as foul play.

Once you've accumulated your case file and feel confident enough in your findings you may feel like going on to the next stage, which is the physical part of the investigation. Depending on the type of investigators you and your team are (if you have one), do you go fully kitted with more technology than an electronics department store or are your more of a traditionalist, opting for a less intrusive approach with items such as dowsing rods, pendulums and trigger objects?

Always remember this is nothing like you see on the TV: there's a good chance nothing at all will happen and you could be sat in a cold, dark, and even damp place for hours on end with nothing to show for it. Don't be disheartened. This is par for the course. The programmes you see on TV or online are highlights pasted together from what could be hours and hours of footage, and edited into either an half hour or hour program, which gives the impression that all Hell has been let loose; when realistically, the experience could be flat as road-kill. What's more, these programs don't always do detailed research; in some cases, they dig just deep enough to give basic information in order to keep the viewer interested, especially if the location has a notorious past such as imprisonment, murder and especially torture. When investigating areas that you have seen on a show it is tempting to go on the information they have shared, but by doing your own legwork, there's a good chance you may pick up on something has others have missed, and it's details like that what will give you credibility, which unfortunately at the moment is in short supply within paranormal quarters.

If you are lucky enough to encounter any sort of paranormal occurrences on your all -night vigils, it is imperative you document all that you can, for you have become the witness to the events. It then becomes up to you to share with others, if you so wish, your findings. If you are using items such as video and sound recorders, review your footage as soon as you can, and also get others to double check and verify what you have found, as there is always a good chance you may have missed or misinterpreted the information, and having a second pair of eyes go over your work can be very useful. If your work is client-based, you must alert them to any findings and experiences, and also respect their wishes on whether or not they wish to go public. When going into an investigation, you must acknowledge that there is a good chance they might want to keep it between you and themselves. This is important, and I cannot stress it enough, _**you must respect their wishes!**_ There is nothing worse than a so-called paranormal investigation team promising trust and respect only to go to the newspapers at the earliest opportunity, looking for instant fame. It doesn't work like that, because this is your reputation: and once you get that kiss-and-tell reputation against the wishes of those who have asked you for help, no one will take you seriously. Unfortunately, there are plenty out there like that.

Going back to client-based investigations. Always give a detailed account of your findings even if nothing has happened, even if it turns out to be simply natural phenomena, be truthful. Don't exaggerate or play down incidents, and more so let your clients know that if at anytime during the investigation they are unsure or have any additional questions, you will be more than willing to answer them and not distance yourself; and even after you have packed up and gone, leave contact details in case a follow up investigation is needed.

MORE FOOL YOU TECHNOLOGY

Regardless of what anyone tells you there are no items on the technology market made specifically to look for or detect ghosts. On the other hand there are products which have been adapted solely for the purpose of searching for signs of the afterlife, but their creation is questionable due to the fact these items started life as something else.

Don't get me, wrong I'm not saying not to use technology, because in some areas it's brilliant. It is just important to remember that items such as EMF readers, also known as a K2 (see below) are primarily used to detect physical elements that you cannot see to aid in DIY.

Over the years many would be paranormal investigators and public ghost hunting groups have spent what I can only imagine on securing what they believe to be the holy grail of ghost hunting equipment hoping it will give them the edge over any competition especially in the case of public ghost hunting companies but because of these items being commercially accessible to anyone no one has the edge over anyone else so in the terms of chess champions it's become stalemate if anything the only way results differ is because of the way they are being used. As mentioned above, one of the most popular electronic items for paranormal enthusiasts to buy is a small handheld device called the K2. This simple device has been reinvented with ghost hunters in mind.

This device measures and locates electromagnetic fields, in particular extremely low frequencies, but is limited in its capabilities. It then registers its findings by five coloured lights on the front of the casing, the colour representing the frequency level, giving the user a visual reading. Because of this, it is favoured by ghost hunters since it can be used quite easily in the dark. Although this product is aimed at paranormal enthusiasts and marketed as such there is nothing in the design to make it exclusively paranormal for there are many other variations of electromagnetic field radiation detectors available to buy especially for those where microwave and electronic shielding or detection is required.

The same can also be said for cameras. A few years ago, there seemed to be a fad of removing the internal hot filter in cameras, thus enabling higher sensitivity in the IR region of the light spectrum, giving what ghost hunters believed a better chance of photographing and actual ghost, as regular cameras weren't having much luck with the task. It isn't that they weren't up to the task, it's more a question of the subject matter - I mean how do you take a photo of an object with no physical mass? To capture an image on a camera there has to be a solid subject in the first place, even smoke has mass. .

Don't get me wrong, I'm not dismissing technology altogether. One area it can be useful in is in the audio department, in the form of EVPs, electronic voice phenomenon, these are voices or other sounds that are found on electronic audio recorders, tape recorders or Dictaphones, or even computer equipment on which have been unintentionally recorded. For example sounds can be picked up unknowingly on all sorts of devices similar to how images can be captured on camera that were at the time invisible to the human eye. In my opinion if you are wanting to capture any sort of paranormal phenomena audio is probably the best way to go, not only is it a very easy format to use it is also very friendly on the pocket and no special equipment is required, apart from a single device To do this, you can use either one of the two best methods: first, leaving the recording device running in a locked off and secured area for an allotted amount of time and then checking frequently for results, or secondly, use the recorder as an aid by calling out controlled questions and leaving gaps between those questions to see if those same gaps get filled by audible responses on your device: it's as simple as that.

Another electronic device which can be useful within paranormal quarters are temperature loggers. These devices measure the ambient temperature of an object or environment where the equipment is set up or stored, and can be quite useful when it comes to investigations; this is because it has been said on more than one occasion that where hauntings are prevalent so are temperature fluctuations, and even though you may not see or hear an actual ghost it doesn't mean there isn't one present, for hauntings are not only noted by vision but also by smell and temperature.

One item in particular I must not forget to mention is with regard to the previous subject of EVP and voices captured on electronic recording devices. The item to which I refer goes by a few names but is best known as a "ghost box". Basically, the ghost box is nothing but a broken radio which moves through radio frequencies and picks up random radio waves, which can give whoever uses it the impression they are receiving real-time intelligent answers. To be honest, I for one am not convinced that this is so.

The ghost box is a standard radio with a frequency scanning function (the part that scans for stations) that has been disabled, so when it finds a station it is unable stop on it, and simply carries on to the next, permanently jumping through its available frequencies snatching sounds from transmissions, static and white noise then added to some well timed questions by the handler, the information is interpreted with a little help from pareidolia and a little bit of imagination as communication from the other side.

One thing I have noticed on the public ghost hunts which I have attended is everyone has with them a mobile phone, in most cases a smart-phone. The majority of event organisers, at some point before the start of the event, will ask everyone to turn off their mobile phones, not just because of the chance of it ringing every two minutes (there is nothing worse than being sat in silent vigil disturbed by someone's notification tone) but because these devices are constantly giving off a signal, thus interfering with items such as EMF readers and causing false readings. Even putting it on aeroplane mode or silent doesn't stop it giving off a signal so, for me a mobile phone on an investigation or public ghost hunt must be fully turned off without a doubt: remember a mobile phone is there to contact the living not the dead.

As a researcher I have spent most of my adult life searching for the exact same answers as everyone else within this field, and like most genuine investigators who have chosen a similar path, am still waiting for that day or night when there arrives the opportunity to witness and record such occurrences. The lack of evidence at the moment is in favour of proving two possible outcomes: firstly, there is nothing out there to capture, or secondly, we are going about things the wrong way with regards to investigating this phenomena. In my opinion the lack of credible evidence is down to our dependence on the technology we use and, in some cases, incorrectly. To witness such phenomena a person needs to connect spiritually and you cannot do that with batteries and flashing lights, for that connection a person needs to be at one with the products of their trade by making them personal to the user by using their own inner energies that many have forgotten they possess because of their dependence of mass produced technologies which they believe will make their lives easier.

Don't get me wrong I'm not against technology if it's used correctly. But from what I have experienced, and what I have used myself within the paranormal field, it is better off being used elsewhere.

Ever since early man first stepped out of his cave armed with no more than a bit of flint and a rudimentary sharpened stick he has forever been recognised as the hunter; the one who faced danger on a daily basis, not because he wanted to but because he had to due to his very existence being dependent on his skill to outwit something he feared.

As time went by early man's achievements grew, but so did his ability to manipulate his surroundings by integrating what he discovered into how he hunted, making him more efficient; and the less he hunted the more he could put his energies into other avenues, giving rise to other stages of human evolution, such as the bronze and iron ages right up to the industrial age, jumping to where we are today. The main reason early man got us to where we are today is because of his ability to understand that tools can make his life easier, and the better the tool, the less effort he has to put into the actual job. Not only that, he understood that by going down this path made his quests less dangerous.

Now we can't blame our prehistoric ancestors for wanting to make their lives easier because it cannot have been an easy life for them and what they did took a huge amount of effort and skill even with their basic tools. Compared to those days we have it so much easier, for one thing, we don't have to go out and hunt down our lunch or deal with the fear of knowing that our dinner might actually eat us.

Today we have so much technology at our disposal, which isn't all bad because on the side of safety and medicine which will only be of benefit. But on the other hand it can make us lazy; As I stated earlier a tool is meant to *assist* us, not do the job for us: otherwise what is the point of the human element in this equation?

Ghost hunting is an area which is a prime example of misused apparatus because it seems many people who partake in paranormal activities are under the pretext that simply buying a piece of equipment, such as a ghost box, will bear fruit immediately, but realistically that is not the case. No matter what anyone says, there is no equipment on the market that has specifically been created to detect ghosts or spirits, only adaptations of devices made for other purposes. It is impossible for an individual or company to create a piece of equipment designed to detect an entity that no one knows the elements of which they consist. Remember the tools which you use will only assist you, and not do the job for you. That is where many are failing: they are unwittingly falling into the trap of purchasing such items because they have seen similar devices used, with very positive results, on the TV or online shows. Just remember what works for one doesn't necessarily mean it will work for all.

Don't get me wrong, I'm not saying you shouldn't use technology in your quest, just be aware of its original purpose. I've made those mistakes myself, have been there and done that, and realised I've spent a lot of time, money and effort on items that, for me, don't serve a purpose. In fact the only modern technology I use now are a camera and torch (flashlight), because I believe that what I use must not be powered by batteries but by my own senses. I have turned a corner with regards to my own investigating and ghost hunting techniques, and gone back in time to an era that isn't distracted by flashing lights and items that forever need charging and can be manipulated by Wifi signals.

A small case measuring forty two inches by eleven and a half inches with a depth of five and a half inches and held together by no more than leather and metal studs with a worn leather handle is the Victorian era case that carries all that I use, no need for batteries or charging points: everything I need is ready at a moments notice.

Contents are as follows: one room thermometer, because as we all know temperature fluctuations are a sure sign of ghostly activity. One old brass compass, to be used in place of EMF readers such as a K2. One old silver mechanical pocket watch, being able to monitor times and dates are a staple of any investigation. A variation of silver and brass bells attached to ribbons and cord, to be placed in areas of activity after it has been checked and ruled out for traffic and draughts, which results in ringing once disturbed. One brass pendulum; being brass it's a perfect conductor for spiritual activity and can aid in divination and dowsing practises as well, as being a tool used for locating gold, water and oil due to the belief that the pendulum works similar to an aerial or antenna picking information from purported energies emanating from objects or even individuals on a subconscious level. One pair of brass and copper dowsing rods, which work on a similar principle to the pendulum, but these are more widely used and are more mobile, as well as being a popular choice amongst novices due to the success rate amongst all the divination tools. Candle holders and candles, which are used as a light source as well as being good trigger objects, allowing the spirits to move the flames, as well being brilliant in areas such as séances and scrying. Due to health and safety regulations many locations no longer allow the use of candles but there are still many locations that will still allow them under supervision.

Collection of old coins, old pennies from the Edwardian and Victorian eras to be used as trigger objects. An old bible and small wooden cross. The use of a Bible is down to the preference of the user, due to their beliefs and can be used for comfort or even as an aid to investigation by the reading of passages, the cross can also be used as a trigger object. Old brass magnifying glass, quite a unique one that can be used in an array of ways if you're a budding Sherlock Holmes, but I use it as a trigger object and also for visual temperate tests by checking the moisture or fog on the lens. Notebook and pencil: the good old notebook and pencil to keep accurate notes as you go along - you could use a pen but there's less chance of a pencil leaking. Another little item added is a little bit more modern and that is a triple lens 8mm movie camera that is manually wound, and works as good as the day it was made; the film used can be purchased and converted by companies found locally or online, or if you are into your photography you could have a go yourself. Not forgetting, every now and then depending on your audience or client a spirit board session, and even though many people frown upon, this practice it's actually uses the same technique as using a pendulum or dowsing rods.

It isn't that going old school will work for everyone, some will still prefer to work with technology as aids, but since building up this small collection, I've had better results than I have with modern techniques. This is perhaps because I am quite old fashioned when it comes down to it, and I strongly believe a person should be aided by the tools they use and not distracted by them.

If something is worthwhile, surely it's worth the effort for example if you are not going to give it your very best what is the point of doing it in the first place?

THE PARANORMAL AND SOCIAL MEDIA PLATFORMS

For most of my adult life, I have had an interest in the paranormal, starting with collecting stories from friends and colleagues to buying books to add to my ever increasing collection, and for one minute even thought about broadcasting my interests to the outside world. I was happy doing my own little thing in my own little paranormal world. I have never been one for computers; no disrespect to anyone, but I have never seen why anyone would spend most of their free time sat in front of a screen when there is a vast wide world out there waiting to be explored. Everyone needs to get out and feel the wind and fresh air on their faces. Well in my opinion, they do, anyway.

I have always been aware of online social media platforms such as Facebook but never really gave them much attention, until a day when I had a little free time and decided to explore this online world. Admittedly, this was mainly because I was looking for a particular item and was recommended to a local selling group. So I set myself up a profile and went shopping. Not only did I find more or less what I wanted, but I also realised there were groups for more or less everything; from cars and motorbikes, military to collectables, help and support groups, and all the way through to the paranormal and the unexplained. As I mentioned earlier, I am no more qualified than the next person in this field, but I do possess a logical head and am quite methodical in my work - so I decided to work on creating my own online paranormal group built on the basis of sharing stories and experiences, as well as letting those with similar interests advertise and promote their own work and interests on the group without them needing to pay an advertising fee. About a week or so later, BRF Paranormal Facebook page was born and open to everyone's scrutiny.

It's thanks to the creation of the group that I have been involved in some brilliant projects, including being invited as a special guest on a few public ghost hunts, to which I am very grateful and thankful. I have also appeared as a guest on a few paranormal radio shows

Being in the public eye, especially in the paranormal, your motives and style become open to scrutiny and you acquire a reputation for yourself, whether you want one or not. Luckily the one I have is hopefully of respect, as I like to treat others as I wish to be treated: That applies to both living and dead. Unfortunately, not everyone I have met in paranormal circles shares this desire to maintain a decent and honest reputation, and sadly are those within the paranormal world who simply don't care about furthering their paranormal understanding, and see it only as a way to find quick and easy fame, as well as filling their pockets along the way.

Over the last few years, those that have closely followed the ins and outs of what's happening in the paranormal world (especially those that enjoy the public events side of things) will have noticed the amount of groups that have emerged. Most have also noticed that they all seem to cover the same locations, and very rarely offer anything new. There are also a large number of groups who try to keep locations exclusive, denying other groups access so they can monopolise it. Having such a large variation of groups isn't always a bad thing: It can be beneficial to the paying public, because if numerous groups cover a particular location that is popular then customers can choose the one that favours their pocket or go for the one that is most reputable. On the other hand, it also shows that if one group can sell tickets for around £35 and another sell theirs, for the same venue, at £50, it can highlight the amount of profit that team is attempting to make, and whether or not financial gain is their main incentive. Playing devil's advocate, though, it is important to remember that groups have to pay venue costs, staff costs, catering (if they provide food during the event), as well as trying to refund the costs of equipment purchased – so just because one team charges more than another doesn't mean they're prices are unreasonable.

A majority of public events are advertised online through groups such as mine, and a large percentage of these very groups do it for the right reasons: that is to say, they give the paying customer the experience of being a ghost hunter for the night and a chance to explore some locations that the general public wouldn't normally get access to, and I applaud those groups out there who only want the best for their customers.

Be aware though, even though most public event groups are genuine there are those that sneak in through the net who are not so customer-focused, and their aim is to simply make money, without caring how they get it or where or who it comes from. Such groups, however, are difficult to spot until it is too late and they've disappeared with your money. Luckily, this doesn't happen often but it does happen. The preferred method for this type of scam is to advertise an already popular location at a reasonable (but not too cheap) price using a date that is not too distant, so those expecting a decent night out don't have to wait too long. In most cases the event location is never booked by the so-called "event-organisers": It has even been known for those that have paid for tickets to turn up at the event location, ready for a night of ghost-hunting and fun, only to be told no such bookings ever even existed. Even worse when it comes to trying to get some sort of refund, explanation, or even retribution. Usually, these scam-organisers have disappeared and closed down all social media accounts by that point. On a positive, if paying through either Paypal or credit card, you at least get a better chance of a refund.

When booking an event such as this, go by recommendations by family and friends, and I would always recommend to research companies before booking with them. Read their reviews, Google the team's name, and look to see if the people involved have had a lot of paranormal-event businesses with different names – if a team is repeatedly changing their name, then it is likely they are trying to shake off a bad reputation. If you do still have concerns, you could always contact the location owners directly to give you a total piece of mind.

Even though there is a lot of negativity within the realm (which does thankfully comes from only a very small minority), the vast majority of people I've come across are genuine, decent people, who are happy to help each other, and who realise that the paranormal field is more than about making money or getting the most social media likes and publicity.

Another disadvantage of the paranormal within social media is the simple fact there is a lot of rubbish to sift through. What with all the conspiracy theories and theorists, and those who seem to believe in absolutely nothing but yet spend time on paranormal pages, mostly ridiculing those who do believe in it. Another thing to look out for are the live streamers who use the platform to try to self promote, trying to make a name for themselves rather than spending time investigating hauntings, doing nothing but talk throughout what is supposed to be an investigation with the camera focused on them. Now, I'm not saying that all live streamers are like this: I have watched quite a few who are genuine, who are happy to debunk their own experiences when evidence shows it to be more rational. But there are a few out there with motives other than searching for ghosts. My advice to you is you are intent on spending time in the online paranormal world, is keep your circle tight and stick to individuals you either know or have been recommended by those you have faith in; there are a lot of egos out there and if you are not careful, they will try to draw you into their circle and twist you with their sense of celebrity-filled ideology

I'm not trying to scare you away from the online paranormal world: far from it. All I'm saying is, be careful, and try not to let what others tell you cloud your judgement. Always stay true to yourself and keep your intentions honest, especially within the paranormal because it can be so easy to be swayed. The online paranormal world can be a wonderful place to be if you let it, and you can come into contact with some brilliant people share your interests. During the public ghost hunts I've attended, I've come into contact with some wonderful people whom I would never have met if not for the paranormal, some who have become very close friends. So, the online world is not all bad, you can make it what you want it to be; as the saying goes "you reap what you sow".

What's more it can be a great platform for getting your work noticed in its own merit. It is because of my involvement with the online community that I, as I mentioned previously, had the opportunity to share my views and thoughts on the airwaves. Primarily, in the form of a guest on online paranormal radio shows, and leading me to interviewing some of the world's most recognised people from the paranormal realm, not only from the UK but worldwide, in the form of co-host on our own radio show.

PARANORMAL RADIO

It's funny where paths can take you. When I first involved the general public with my paranormal views and interests via my online group, I never dreamed I would become involved in sharing my opinions and interviewing worldwide guests as a radio host.

It all started when I was invited by who is now a very good friend, Tom Warrington, onto his reasonably-new online radio show *The Pure Paranormal Radio Show*, aired through a radio station called *Pulse Talk Radio*.

Tom was looking for guests who, in their own unique way, have an involvement with the paranormal, and because of my BRF Paranormal group and what he'd researched about me, invited me on as a guest on his show. I was asked to be a guest not just once but three times, after which Tom contacted me one evening and kindly offered me the role of co-host on his show. In its first year, the show won a prestigious award for best paranormal radio show at a paranormal conference, and, before you know, it four years have almost past but to clarify I have been part of the show for only three and a half of those years because I joined Tom as co-host in the second half of its first year and all credit must go to Mr Warrington for creating such a wonderful and down to earth show which in my opinion doesn't get the credit it deserves. In fact it's become so popular that the show not only streams through *Pulse Talk Radio* but also another radio station known as *Fantasy Radio,* which streams the show simultaneously.

Each and every week, we interview guests - some famous, some not, but each as fascinating as each other, and all from the comfort of our own homes, via Skype. The funny thing about all this is that, even though Tom and I get along so great, we had been broadcasting the show a year before we met each other in person.

As previously mentioned, the show is aired from our respective homes: Tom in Lincolnshire and myself in the town of Doncaster, South Yorkshire. And our guests? Well it could be from anywhere in the world, not just the UK. In fact, we've had quite a few guests from the United States take part in the show, our guests very kindly setting aside time for us despite the varying time differences between us, which is very much appreciated, especially since everyone these days is trying to juggle work and social time, which is not always easy.

As we've already established, the show goes out live once myself and Tom have linked up and connected with our guest, or sometimes guests, and its live for the next hour and a half. This isn't without its problems, mainly due to occasional connection issues, as Skype can be very temperamental: one minute brilliant the next an absolute sod. And it never seems to be location-specific, for we've had guests who live only a few miles away have a terrible connection, whereas guests on the other side of the planet have a connection so clear they could have been next door.

Connection issues aside, the only other downside of going live is that sometimes the odd swear word pops into the conversation, especially when we are talking about a subject which we are passionate about, or has either touched a nerve or needs deep discussion. This is especially true if wrongdoing is involved. The swearing is never intentional, but as we all know sometimes passions flair and they just spurt out.

There is no limit as to what we will talk about. It could be anything involving the paranormal, because each show is based around the specific guest and the questions are based on the field in which they participate. For example, if we are interviewing a ufologist the questions will be based around UFOs, abductions and other aspects regards ufology; or for those who have been involved in production or TV, the questions may be based around their previous work and findings. Questions are always set around our guests, as well as respectfully delving into subjects such as why they do what they do, what their personal beliefs are regarding their findings and experiences. We always research our guests prior to the live show, it's the least we can do for them sharing their time with us.

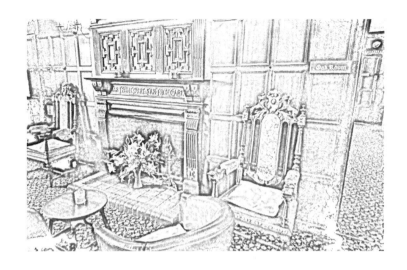

DID YOU HEAR THAT?

At some point on either a ghost hunt or on a paranormal TV show or live stream, you will most probably hear someone say "Did you hear that?" or "I heard someone call my name, di you?", and the reply they often receive when asking that question, is "no". One possible reason why nobody else heard it is not because it's the other side calling us, but because of the ailment known as tinnitus.

Many individuals believe the main symptom is a ringing or humming in the ears, which is true, but that is only one common symptom. Millions of people worldwide suffer from tinnitus and some aren't even aware they have the infliction, whereas others suffer greatly in the form of auditory hallucinations. As I mentioned earlier, tinnitus can come in the form of either a humming, tonal sound of any pitch or even pulsing and clicking sounds, but in many instances it can also appear in form of what we believe are voices calling us, meaning that only the person with the condition can hear it.

There is nothing wrong with the people who suffer from tinnitus, the condition can be brought on by more or less anything, such as prescription drugs, prolonged exposure to loud sounds, and even sleep deprivation: this last is especially relevant because as we all know, most ghost hunts take place overnight; and for those who are just being introduced to their first investigations will find out it can have an extreme effect on our body clocks, especially when done regularly.

Other medical conditions, such as migraines, can also produce similar effects. Migraines especially have been known to trigger such audio and visual illusions (another reason why client medical history needs to be taken prior to investigations. So if you are on your own or on a ghost hunt, and hear your name being called or words spoken to you, more so if no one else seems to have heard the same thing, it doesn't mean the spirits are calling you or you are losing your mind it could be something as simple as a mild case of tinnitus.

A REALISATION

So we've established that there is a side to the paranormal that not everyone sees, a side they don't share with you on TV or in books, but it is a side people must be made aware of. I've not raised the issues to put you off, but to give you a realistic view of what you could be faced with. I believe that it is the duty of those who have had experience in their chosen areas to help guide those who are new to it, to give them the benefit of your victories and mistakes, so they are more prepared. First you must know what lies ahead and what obstacles await you, and once you've established that it is then up to you what your next steps are should you choose to accept the task laid out. And if you do believe it's for you, try to be unique in your approach and walk in no one's shadow dare to be that little bit different and set an example to those that follow.

Be true to yourself and it will show in your work!

In life everyone has an opinion, more so within the paranormal for no two individuals think exactly alike, and it is that individuality that makes the realm so interesting. Granted, not everyone may share your views because you will always get those that, no matter what evidence you submit, will remain sceptical and never be convinced. But, you need to ask yourself who are you trying to convince in the first place, and why is it so important? If you are lucky enough to encounter a paranormal occurrence, for you that is all the evidence you need. Trying to convince a third party is a totally different story. This is mainly because they didn't witness the encounter and in their eyes, and it is sometimes difficult to believe something, especially in the paranormal realm where there are so many fake 'evidence', if you didn't witness it personally. To some, proving their encounter isn't necessary because they are content with what they experienced, but there are those out there who purposely seek that validation of their next encounter, and go to great lengths to capture what they believe to be credible evidence. This can often lead to mistaking natural phenomena for paranormal, which can be easy to do, especially if you've spent an entire night in total darkness, where your senses are heightened due to your lack of vision your other senses kick in; it is so easy to let your imagination get the better of you. Be methodical in your work and question yourself often, and eliminate possibilities by adopting a sceptical attitude whilst you investigate your surroundings.

Depending on the style of investigator you wish to be will determine how much time you spend on an investigation, because there are those who prefer to go in blind where knowledge of location and experiences are concerned, whereas others do background research beforehand. Many say having such knowledge ahead of time alters your expectations and influences your results, but on a personal note, I myself prefer to have prior information so that I can set up accordingly: I do this mainly as I don't see the point of spending six hours in an area where no known activity has ever been reported, whereas that same amount of time can be put to constructive use if you have prior information on a particular route or location of said apparitions.

If you wish to go down the path of background research, there are quite a few credible ways in which to so. For example, there is the internet, but do be wary as a lot of information that is online may not necessarily be accurate or even of first hand accounts, and possibly copied; and as we know whispers from one ear to another can sometimes alter a story so much so that it becomes unrecognisable from its origins. I'm not saying all information online has become corrupted, because you sometimes can find some great snippets of information – I am just cautioning you to be wary of its source. You will come across many that choose this way of retrieving the information they require because it's probably the easiest way and requires very little effort, and these days can be done almost anywhere thanks to modern smartphones and tablets.

One of my favourite forms of acquiring information is through books. To me, a book is a more satisfying way of acquiring the information I require and I know that the information within those pages has more likely been scrutinised by the very person who published it, and in many cases is unique to that publication. Another way of acquiring information is the good old fashioned way of talking to people, known as eyewitnesses, these people are imperative when it comes to researching sightings and hauntings. Don't just talk to witnesses though, talk to neighbours and if possible those that work in and around the area: chances are they may hold what could be vital information to you.

WHAT ABOUT THE GHOST STORIES?

Ok, we've established that the paranormal realm does not always see the proverbial light, and whatever its faults can be an exciting place to venture and you cannot have the word "paranormal" without ghosts and ghost stories. More so, if the stories are based on true accounts, because who doesn't love a good old fashioned true ghost story?

If you went around the streets and asked a percentage of people if they know of or have been told a ghost story at some point in their life, I believe that a large percentage of those people will probably answer yes, whether they believe in ghosts or not. It's these kind of stories that stick in the minds of all who hear them, especially if you were a child when you first heard a tale of an headless horseman or grey lady I have such a true tale that I will share a little later with you.

No matter where you live there is a very good chance that somewhere nearby is either an haunted building of some sort, be it a residential house, a workplace or in many instances an old stately type home; even if it's not an house or a building as such, it is possible there is a piece of land that plays host to a haunting, and where I live is no different.

Doncaster is in the South Yorkshire region of the United Kingdom, and started life as a Roman settlement that was known as Danum. Jump forward a few hundred years after the Romans had departed to what we know as the middle ages, and Doncaster as it now known became a busy market town. In the year 1204, Doncaster suffered a catastrophic fire due to most of the buildings consisting of no more than wood and other combustible materials, more or less destroying overnight what had taken years to create. Further forward a couple of hundred years more as the town kept ever growing, witnessed on more than one occurrence of plague, and even though the population was more or less wiped out the community rebuilt and continued to increase. That is just a small portion of the history of this town, so there alone you have layers of history and as you know with history comes ghosts and, Doncaster does have its fair share.

The following accounts are concerning the areas in and around Doncaster, some may sound familiar to you, others not so much, but to my knowledge all are true to account starting with one I witnessed myself.

THE BROWN BOOT

A few years back, Doncaster Racecourse, the home of the famous St Leger, every Sunday used to play host to a huge car boot sale, which I frequently attended. At the time, it was one of the biggest in the country, so did get very busy. If you had a stall or were selling as a casual, you had to queue at a particular stretch of road and wait in line - but to ensure that you got a decent pitch, you had to get in line very early, often around 5 am and then wait until 7 am when the gates opened But I didn't mind the early starts, because once I'd gotten my place in the line, I would turn off my engine and read a book. On this particular summer's morning, after packing my trusty little Skoda the night before, I set off from my home, which was approximately ten minutes away from the racecourse

On approach to the final stretch of road known as, Leger Way, to the left is a school complex and between the school and the road is a large grassy area which leads to some bushes and fences that border the racecourse complex. Driving that particular morning was very uneventful up to this point, the sky was clear and visibility was reasonably good and I was in good spirits (pardon the pun) and in good health. I proceeded to drive down this particular stretch of road. To the left and coming towards me I noticed just above ground level what I thought was either a rabbit, a rat or even a low flying bird and before I knew it, it was passing in front of my car. To my amazement, it wasn't what I thought: what I witnessed was, in fact, the manifestation of what I would describe as a brown leather boot (the right one in case you were wondering); One thing I did notice, though, as it passed in front of me was that even though it did seem solid, I could partially see through. Before I could question myself about it, it reached the other side of the road it had completely vanished.

All that day I questioned myself, trying to understand what I had encountered and replaying it in my head. And you know what? Even to this day, I still cannot describe what I witnessed to be anything else but a brown boot.

WELLS ROAD

Wells Road is an unassuming road in the Wheatley area of Doncaster, and until around two years ago I lived about three streets away from it. The road itself is your typical Doncaster street, a mix of houses and reasonably new bungalows, each with its own little bit of garden and if, you're lucky, a little bit of a parking space.

Before the bungalows were built, stood flat-roofed houses, which, even though built to a budget, served their purpose until finally being demolished and replaced by the bungalows. The rumour was that Wells Road got its name because of allegedly being the location of three wells that supplied the long gone Wheatley Hall with water. Further rumours from way back, mention of poor unfortunates suspected of being witches (which cannot be verified because there are no known documented witch cases in Doncaster) being cast down large wells and crevices in the area that is now known as Wells Road. As mentioned, there is no proof to collaborate this story, but stories do originate from somewhere, so who knows? And to add to the tale, this street was the target of poltergeist activity at more than one property only a few years back, which stopped just as suddenly as it arrived.

When I lived in the area I did speak to one resident of the street, and she told me of some unusual activity when she first moved in to the house. She was sensible in her approach to what she could only describe as the image of an old woman at the top of the stairs; as she explained to me, she had been quite stressed because of the move and the house was still strange to her, for she had not yet had the time to put her mark on it. She never saw the image of the woman again but she did mention at times she did get the sensation that there was someone walking around on the landing, but she learned to live with it.

SOMETHING FROM THE SIXTIES
BRODSWORTH HALL

Brodsworth Hall is situated on the outskirts of Doncaster, has to be one of the most complete and original examples of Victorian architecture in the country. The house in particular was built between 1861 and 1863 for Charles Sabine Thellussion, and was built on a broad limestone ridge which has seen evidence of occupancy since the Iron Age, and running along that ridge is a major route north used by the Romans whose nearby garrison evolved and became what we now know as Doncaster. The hall itself isn't without its share of ghosts and paranormal activity, for it has been reported that the manifestation of what people believe was the original owner has been seen within the buildings walls.

Another sighting is of a lady wearing what has been described as Victorian dress, descending the staircase and disappearing before she reaches the bottom. There are also reports of a male figure wearing a khaki uniform, most probably from the first world war who also appears at the top of the same staircase who when spotted stares coldly at the observer before slowly turning and walking into a nearby room, where when followed leaves no trace of his visit. There are others too, not in visual form, but of sense for many female members of staff have reported that in certain upstairs rooms they have felt the sensation of being pushed in the back as if being ushered by an invisible pair of hands.

These are accounts from within the building, but there are also reports of activity from outside of the building as well. A friend of mine told me of an account he experienced as a child back in the 1960s.

He and a friend had been exploring the grounds, but still in eye-line of the main house, when he and his friend had caught the attention of a man and a woman walking arm in arm along an opposite path. Fearing that they might be in trouble they stopped talking to each other and started walking side by side at a steady pace. He mentioned that the woman's arm uncoupled itself from her male chaperone's, it was at that moment my friend said he felt most uncomfortable and scared. The man, who was wearing what seemed like a dark coloured suit and a hat, suddenly turned his entire body towards and he realised that neither the man or woman seemed to be in contact with the path. What scared them even more was that when they turned round to make sure they weren't being chased, they could see no trace of the couple. My friend then explained to me that he and his friend have never run so fast since that day.

DONCASTER'S LESSER KNOWN OCCURRENCES

As I've previously noted, Doncaster as a town is steeped in history and you cannot have hauntings without history. Luckily we have both. Doncaster's history, like all history, is layered one on top of the other. For example the Romans settled by building a fort naming it Danum and establishing a foothold, jump forward to the 12th century by now the Romans have long gone but the town is now an established market town and to give it more credentials King Richard I gives the town which is now named Doncaster a charter. Further on, the town is almost wiped out by a huge fire but is soon rebuilt. Further still, and the plague strikes the town not just once but three times and in all cases residents that succumb to the disease were hastily disposed of. To give you an idea of the severity of the situation in 1583 virtually all burials between winter and autumn of that year were identified as victims of the epidemic over 800 in total according to records, this is just one small portion of what Doncaster since its birth has had to face, so is there any wonder there are still some unsettled former residents reluctant to leave what they considered home?

The town centre has over the years had its share of spooky goings on, from the sighting of a woman who walks around the market area to incomprehensible voices being heard both inside and outside the Corn Exchange building. This last one is not so surprising, as the bodies of past residents still lay under its foundation; and although the bodies have been blessed before being covered over again, it's no wonder that there's still a strange atmosphere there.

Doncaster Mansion House is a grade one listed building which was officially opened in 1749, and also has its resident ghost in the form of a tall thin gentleman who likes to make his presence felt when important guests are being entertained, and on rare occasions has been seen admiring the paintings that hang on the walls.

It's not just public areas and buildings that see activity. There are also workplaces and residential areas, too. Wheatley Hall Road is a huge stretch of road and is considered a main vein when it comes to serving the needs of the town. Amongst the car showrooms and business parks, that are mentions of a small brown dog that walks in the area, which is believed to have been hit by a car in the days before it became a dual carriageway. On that same stretch of road is a building that I once worked at, although now is under a different ownership, where the restless spirit of a man in a blue boiler suit is still seen going about his business.

Even the house I live in currently still plays host to a previous occupant who passed away in the house, making his presence known on occasion. It does make you wonder about how many people have lived in your house before you and how many passed away in that very same building you live your life and sleep in. More than that, do they realise they've passed over?

In Marshgate, not far from the old North bridge, stands an old warehouse where figures, lights and sounds have been seen and experienced from the top floor by people passing, and one account from a few years back by a jogger tells of an encounter with a woman in a long cream dress carrying an umbrella who seemed to glide rather than walk.

Sandall Beat woods is located just a short distance from the racecourse, and on a good day is a nice place to walk or cycle round; but after dark seems to take on a new persona. Many of those who choose to venture after or near dark experience things such as hearing voices, being touched, along with a general sense of being watched and followed.

WAILING WOODS

Black Carr Plantation, or Wailing Woods as it was known, runs alongside Warning Tongue Lane. The area was originally designed as an exclusive woodland for the local gentry to go hunting, but after changing ownership many times was taken over by the forestry commission in 1953, when its purpose changed to the production of commercial lumber. Even though it changed hands, the general public was still forbidden to use the area until 1994 when the council bought the site.

It was during the eighteenth century that it gained its reputation as the Wailing Wood. The name is linked to a carriage that overturned in fog on the nearby Warning Tongue Lane. It all started when traders selling their wares would use the route on a daily basis; in particular, one couple who had a really productive day and decided to celebrate by sampling the local ale houses, not making their journey home until early evening. By this time, spirits were high and, with a few acquaintances they headed back with a fully loaded cart of barrels and such. By now it was dark and thick fog was drawing in, so by the time they got to Warning Tongue Lane the visibility was practically zero, and this is when tragedy struck: drunk and unable to make sense of things, they guided the horse and cart unintentionally into the ditch, causing a barrel to break loose and killing two men and the horse before catapulting the cart onto the couple. Due to the thick fog, no one was aware of the accident that had just occurred and if not for dying screams of the woman no one would have been any wiser until much later.

Despite best attempts the rescuers knew there was no way they could get the horse off of her in time so sent for a priest, but she died before he could get to the scene. Knowing how bad the carnage was and the difficulty in retrieving the bodies, plus that it was getting light, the rescue party and those involved sent out word to the local parish of the situation. It was then decided for the sake of the local children, so that they wouldn't see the carnage, to bury the bodies where they fell; and with a small service they did just that. Over the years people have claimed to have heard horses and the sound of wooden wheels, along with the sound of what sounds like snapping rope; and every now and then, the sound of a woman screaming along with what can only be described as the smell of ale.

SCOT LANE DONCASTER TOWN CENTRE

This is an account which was referred to me by a third party and after speaking to the individual involved who wishes to remain anonymous thought the story was viable enough to share.

This story goes back to the mid nineteen-eighties and the particular incident involves a gentleman who was at the time in his forties, and in good health. Having been dropped off not too far from the old southern bus station (which is now a car park) at around three in the morning, Peter (not his real name) explained to me his journey through the town took him down Scot lane towards the market area and then home.

His journey was practically uneventful until he got about three quarters down the street, when he explained he could smell horse manure; not just a glimpse on the passing wind, but quite a strong odour, and so strong that he suspected that he'd stepped in something. He checked his shoes only to find nothing, so he carried on his journey. It was then he started to feel uneasy, but he didn't know why. He then heard a horse neighing, followed by the sound of a wooden cart literally a couple of feet away from his position.

He went on to explain that it wasn't a scary encounter because he honestly thought there was a horse and cart behind him. Even when it turned out to be nothing, he put it down to tiredness and he carried on his journey. He told his wife the story who asked him why would you imagine a horse and cart, let alone the smell of manure? It was she who suggested he may have encountered a sort of ghostly replay or even a time slip. Whatever it was that he experienced early that morning, no one will probably ever know for sure, not even the individual that experienced it.

A CHILDHOOD EXPERIENCE

This story did not happen in Doncaster - to be honest, I can't remember the location or even the year. All I remember is it is something I experienced as a child.

I do remember it was the big summer holidays, and my name had been put down for a residential activity course for a week but I wasn't too keen on going because I thought I wouldn't know anyone: there were other schools taking part in the scheme too, and it wasn't until I was on the coach that there were four others I did know. The week away wasn't that bad because we were kept busy with outdoor activities and during the evenings it was either board games, TV or doing our own thing. One of those things was storytelling, which included one of our guides telling us that the camp we were in was once a military establishment, catering for the needs of wounded during the first world war. Basically, it was a hospital to help those sent back from the front, and each of the barracks we occupied is where the beds were located, set up very similarly to how they were for us.

One story in particular had evidence to substantiate it. Less than a quarter of a mile away from the camp were the remains of a disused railway track, which we were told supplied the hospital not only with provisions and medical supplies, but also the patients that would use the facilities. We were told about a nurse who not only cared for her patients but also helped carry supplies back and forth, Sadly, she was crushed under an ill-loaded carriage which, when unstrapped, toppled onto her and killed her. For the remainder of the week we put the stories behind us, until our penultimate evening at the site. While we were all in the activity dorm, one of our guides did checks on both the boys and girls dorms to make sure everything was ok, and all of a sudden he came back into the activity area and told us all to go back to our dorms until further notice because he'd seen lights in the vicinity of the old tracks, which were clear as we were in the middle of nowhere, not even in sight of any street lights. Whilst being ushered to our dorms we all saw, myself included, what could only be described as blue-ish- turquoise lights swaying in the area amongst the trees and these lights seemed to be swinging back and forth.

The check from the staff found nothing that could account for these lights, and things went back to normal until around two am, when we were woken by screaming and shouting from one of the site staff. Once everyone was awake, we wanted to know why we'd been woken which the following morning we did indeed find out. The member of staff who had been the cause of the commotion had been escorted home due to an experience he had encountered whilst securing the site the night that we all saw the lights. He had being doing his rounds when walking across from one building to the other (our dorms) and came across a woman who was over six foot tall and wearing some kind of long dress, carrying a long wooden yoke with two lamps glowing a blue light. She seemed stuck to the spot and just looked at him, and then vanished into nothing.

Even though this happened a long time back I still remember that field trip and would love to go back but unfortunately I don't have a clue where it was, all I remember it seemed to take forever to get there on our coach.

ATHRON STREET

Athron Street in itself is quite unique not, because it has a haunting attached to it but because there is no other street in the UK with that name.

Step back in time to the early 2000s before the supermarket that now stands there was built initially stood a small independent tyre fitting company, the type where you simply drove to the premises and had the tyres fitted on your car while you waited. At one point I was there as a customer and whilst waiting, I noted how old the building was which was now serving purpose as a garage. At the time the owner of the garage had reported numerous times that he was having stones and old coins thrown in his direction, even though he was on his own. It is rumoured there is the spirit of a man that haunts the vicinity in which the garage stood. The garage building is no longer there, all that stands there now is a partial wall that adjoins the supermarket car park.

One thing I have wondered is, does any activity still occur? Since spirit activity is recorded as continuing after buildings have long gone it is possible. And if you ever visit this particular area keep an eye out on the ground for any coins, because it may not just be local shoppers that have misplaced them.

LINDHOLME PRISON

Billy Lindholme is what he is now affectionately known as, but in a previous life he was a Polish airman. During WW2, the area which now houses the prison was a base for Wellington bombers and their crews. One fateful day, a returning crew had a disastrous landing overshooting the runway and crashing in nearby marshland, killing all five Polish airmen. Since that day from time to time people venturing that area started reporting accounts of a figure wearing flying gear speaking in a foreign tongue.

During the 1970s the area was excavated and the wreck of a Wellington bomber was discovered along with the remains of four of its crew. It wasn't until the late 1980s that the remains of the fifth crew member was discovered and given a military burial, but reports still speak of the sighting a person wearing what can only be described as full flying gear not only in the area that is now the prison but also the aircraft museum in Doncaster which houses both parts and full aircraft as well as personal effects from those that piloted those machines.

Could these sightings be the same individual or does the spirit of another former pilot wander the corridors of the aircraft museum?

On more than one occasion I have spent time wandering the aircraft museum in total darkness looking for such activity and even though I have encountered some strange occurrences I've yet to encounter our Polish friend. Maybe I'm not looking in the right areas or at the right time or maybe he's simply finally at peace?

MANSION HOUSE, DONCASTER TOWN CENTRE

The Mansion House is a grade 1 listed building which is owned and managed by Doncaster Council, located in the centre of town. This Georgian building was the residence of the Mayor of Doncaster from 1750 to 1922 and was fitted and decorated in such a manor to reflect the importance of its role.

Today it stands as one of only three Mansion Houses in England, and is still used for both civic and private functions such as weddings, afternoon teas and it even plays hosts to open days.

If you are lucky enough to get the chance to explore this building which I have done a couple of times, you may stumble across a very tall man in a long black coat admiring the many paintings on the walls and has also been known to mingle amongst important guests.

The identity of this individual is unknown but some believe it to be the manifestation of a former Mayors personal attendant who still goes about his civic duty.

FRENCHGATE SHOPPING CENTRE

Before the Frenchgate shopping centre came to be, stood a building known as Volunteer Inn. Within that Inn is reputed to reside a ghost that was given the name Cynthia. No one knows why she was given this name or the real identity of this individual; all that is known is that both the landlord and landlady took a liking to this friendly female apparition so much so they gave her an identity. Today stands the shopping centre but it has been reported once in a while when the centre is closed staff have caught glimpses of Cynthia on the ground floor.

PEMBROKE AVENUE BALBY

Some time ago I was given details regarding a private rented residence on this street (to respect the anonymity of anyone who now lives at that address, I won't be supplying the house number in this retelling).

I was given a phone number via a third party with regards to some unusual occurrences that had allegedly been taking place. When I got in touch with the occupier of the house, she told me that every time she went for a bath she got the distinctive feeling that someone was loitering about on the landing, outside the door. Even though she knew her partner was downstairs but when it came to confronting this feeling no evidence of anyone being there ever came to light.

The worst incident she told me of was when she was folding some clothes up in the living room and heard what she thought was a cough coming from the kitchen. At the time her partner had also heard the same sound and confirmed what she had heard; and not just a quick cough but a deep, dry smokers cough. Knowing there could not possibly be anyone else in the house, they quickly ran to the area they believed the sound to have come from only the be greeted by a plastic cereal bowl sitting in the middle of the kitchen floor, and when bending down to pick up the bowl a foul stench of stale tobacco filled their nostrils - which dissipated just as quickly as it first became noticeable. But what followed next really gave them something to think about, because once the cereal bowl had been put back in its place in the overhead cupboard and the door had been shut, they both said to me "hand on heart the cupboard door opened on its own and slammed itself shut right in front of both of us".

After the initial shock of witnessing this, they did invite me round to spend a night there but I was never able to make it. However, they did send me little updates by text mainly with regards to the reoccurring smell of tobacco. Neither one of them smoked and when I asked about any previous furnishings that had been left by the previous occupants that may have retained fragrances, I was told that apart from the kitchen table and wallpaper which they decorated over, the house had been empty.

A couple of months after my last interaction with the couple, they moved to be closer to relatives and I sadly lost contact with them, but the house is still there. It does make me wonder if the latest occupants have had any similar experiences whilst living at that address?

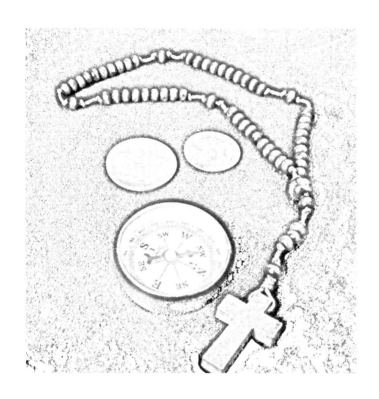

SAVE SOME MONEY WITH AN
ALTERNATIVE TOOLBOX

We all know in this day and age money doesn't go far, what with hard earned pay rises being below the rate of inflation and constant living cost increases hammering our pockets. Ghost hunting if you let it can be an expensive pastime: if you're not careful, you could find yourself spending money better spent elsewhere. What's more, you could find yourself with purchases you don't end up using especially if the very items you have chosen are only because someone has recommended them to you. What works for one doesn't always work for others, so don't be tempted to buy something because it's the next big ghost hunting thing, go with what works for you. And if you want to go down the technology line that's fine, it just may be better to first take the time to learn how items work before buying them, because you will be surprised how many people don't really appreciate or know how what they are using works.

As we all know most ghost hunts are held overnight even though some have been known to have been held during daylight hours - after all, ghostly experiences occur during the day as well. There is one item or tool that no ghost hunter should ever be without and that is a trusty torch (flashlight), because there is a good chance a lot of locations won't be familiar to you, especially at two in the morning. For safety reasons, visibility is paramount, so get yourself a reliable torch. Keeping safety in mind, not just for yourself but for anyone else who may share in your adventures, get yourself a first aid kit, it doesn't have to be fancy just a basic one will do and be confident enough to use not just on yourself but on others too, chances are you will never need it but it's always better to be safe than sorry.

GLOWSTICKS

At some point you will have come across these, and you probably know them even if you've never used them. One snap and they glow for hours, and come in an array of colours. Use these as a backup light source just in case your torch batteries run flat or you have lighting issues. What's more, in unfamiliar locations place them at key points such as exits and clear routes in case you should you need to make an hasty retreat: because they come in a multiple of colours, you can also use them as safety markers warning of dangerous or no go areas, and an added bonus all this light can be bought from your local pound shop.

CHILDREN'S TOYS

No doubt you've heard of trigger objects? An object placed in a controlled environment to entice the curiosity of a spirit, these trigger objects can be anything from coins, religious items such as crosses, and in the case of child spirits, toys: because what child doesn't like playing with toys? Soft toys are such as teddy bears are perfect because these timeless classics, are recognised by all ages no matter what the era they originate from and are good on the pocket because most charity shops will have such donations (and by purchasing from such places you will be helping to support a charity in the process).

OLD RADIOS

If you feel you would like some sort of technology in your kit and don't want or cannot afford to purchase a ghost box or similar, why not opt for a much cheaper option in the form of an old three band radio LW/MW/FM. Use the obsolete LW frequency and because this particular frequency has no or minimal chatter chances are your results will be less tainted by more modern interference.

COMPASS

Many people use items such as the well known K2 to measure EMF readings, although evidence points to them being unreliable, so instead why not simply acquire yourself an inexpensive hiking compass which in itself you will find more reliable and it doesn't rely on batteries to be able to use it.

GOOD OLD NOTEPAD AND PEN

Speaks for itself really: note down any anomalies with time and dates as well as anything else you may wish to add to aid in your quest.

DOWSING RODS

Time old tradition which is still used today and is one of the most cost effective ways of practising divination. They can be used on ghost hunts by way of using the yes/no method simply by asking basic questions, which also applies to pendulums too.

BELLS

How can bells help me search for ghosts, you may ask? Using bells in investigations is a method that is as old as the hills themselves. This cost effective way just needs a few little bells and a few lengths of either ribbon, lace or even string. Tie a length of your lace or ribbon to each bell and place your bells by the ribbon so they dangle freely at intervals in areas of known activity making allowances for draughts and traffic and that's it. Used in a controlled environment these bells will give audible warning of any interference.

CHALK AND POWDER

A very cheap investigative method which is still used today - but be prepared to tidy up after yourself. Simply sprinkled in areas of activity such as on floors, tables and shelf or window ledges any such activity will break the powder layer leaving behind such evidence as fingerprints.

CAMERA

If you wish to search for visual evidence, a camera is a must, but you don't have to break the bank on the latest top range offerings from the top brands: a simple point and shoot is more than sufficient. Look at it this way: all the alleged ghosts that have been caught on camera haven't been captured on professional setups, but your normal everyday mass produced offerings, all it takes is to be in the right place at the right time and for that any camera is better than nothing.

MOBILE PHONE

I know we've mentioned mobile phones previously but this phone serves a different purpose. Everyone these days has some sort of smartphone and being the owner of such a device you will realise that with all the background apps constantly running the battery takes a hammering and may not last a full night even though during investigations they should be turned off, so as a backup keep yourself a cheap pay as you go phone as backup just in case of an emergency or just to let someone know where you are especially if you investigate alone.

WARM CLOTHES, A HAT AND DECENT FOOTWEAR

A necessity on a ghost hunt depending on the time of year and location, be it indoors or outside, is appropriate clothing and footwear. As you are well aware during the night the temperature can plummet even in the warmer months and wearing inappropriate clothes can make four hours feel like eight and if you are not comfortable you are indeed not at your best so don't let the focus of the night take away the importance of your wellbeing.

TRIAL AND ERROR

What you have just read is only an example of what you could do to save a little bit of money, and as you progress you will start to adapt in your approach to investigating, figuring out your own unique methods by experimenting with more or less anything you can lay your hands on. There is absolutely nothing wrong with trying to be different; don't let anyone tell you otherwise. If it works for you then stick to it! After all, what this community needs is more people who are willing to think outside of the box because that is the only way we are going to see any sort of progress.

STAY IN CONTACT

Quite self explanatory really but as you will be going around locations in near pitch black conditions, you need to stay in contact with fellow ghost hunters so the best way to do that is by simple two way radios, or walkie talkies as they're known. Used not just for emergencies these simple devices can be used to usher investigators to the more active locations without the need for shouting your head off.

PERMISSION

It costs nothing, but it is something all ghost hunters must have and is one of the most important aspects of being a ghost hunter: No matter where you go, always ask permission; where possible, get that permission in writing to avoid any legal troubles in regards to trespassing. You need to remember that if a property owner doesn't want you to investigate, they don't have to give a reason and you must respect that decision! Don't go breaking the law by taking matters into your own hands: for all you know, your request could have been denied due to safety reasons and that refusal could inadvertently save your life.

SAFE AND CAUTIOUS

Safety during a ghost hunt is priority, ask any decent public ghost hunting events company and the first thing they will say is no matter how great the location is, safety is first on the list and it should be the same with you. If the location is new to you, prepare yourself with knowledge of its layout beforehand and speak to key-holders with regards to that location's health and safety policy, such as fire escapes and routes. Ghost hunting should be fun not dangerous.

A THANK YOU

Well that's it folks. I know it's not the biggest or most fascinating read that you will have come across but I believe it is an honest and accurate account of what to expect if you decide that the paranormal realm is for you. I wish you well in your venture and if any of the tips that I've mentioned can in any way help you then it will have been worth it, and I thank you for accepting my guidance.

Be true to yourself along with those that seek your guidance and don't be tempted to stray, because as the saying goes "nothing worth the while comes easily", and if your heart is truly in your work then that effort becomes second nature.

Finally, I would like to thank everyone that I have crossed paths with regarding my paranormal work, be it a positive or negative one, because if you don't experience what is wrong with the realm you then don't truly appreciate what is good about it; and as you will discover, there are some good people within its ranks and if your circle includes such people then you wont go far wrong. What's more, these individuals you will find are more than willing to help you out or give you guidance and that is what the paranormal realm should be all about.

Once again I would like to say thank you for taking the time to read my ramblings and even if our paths have never have, or never will be likely to cross, I still wish you well in whatever endeavours you choose to partake.

Happy and safe hunting or investigating.

THOUGHT.

Maybe the afterlife isn't all we believe it to be
and we in fact create our own ghosts aided
only by our inability to let go?

FOOD FOR THOUGHT.

Did you know graveyards and cemeteries are not the same thing?
A graveyard is a cemetery that is located near a church, whereas a cemetery is a freestanding graveyard where no church is present. So just to confuse you a little more, a graveyard is a cemetery but a cemetery is not necessarily a graveyard.

ACKNOWLEDGEMENTS

I would like to, as the author of this work, take the time to acknowledge those that helped and inspired me to create this book and who have made this publication possible.

Starting with my partner, Beth Murray, for her editing and proof reading skills. Also, huge thanks to my daughter, Laura, and sons, Matthew and Daniel, for being such a huge part of my life.

Not forgetting all those from within the paranormal realm with whom I have had either direct or indirect dealings with, because without your influence I wouldn't be the person I am today.

FINAL THOUGHT

If you ever feel like things are getting on top of you, just remember:
A diamond is nothing more than a lump of coal that did well under pressure.

Printed in Great Britain
by Amazon